Resilience

HBR EMOTIONAL INTELLIGENCE SERIES

HBR Emotional Intelligence Series

How to be human at work

The HBR Emotional Intelligence Series features smart, essential reading on the human side of professional life from the pages of *Harvard Business Review*.

Empathy

Happiness

Mindfulness

Resilience

Other books on emotional intelligence from *Harvard Business Review*:

HBR's 10 Must Reads on Emotional Intelligence

HBR Guide to Emotional Intelligence

Resilience

HBR EMOTIONAL INTELLIGENCE SERIES

Harvard Business Review Press

Boston, Massachusetts

Copyright 2017 Harvard Business School Publishing Corporation
All rights reserved
Printed in the United Kingdom by TJ Books Limited

16

The web addresses referenced in this book were live and correct at the time of the book's publication but may be subject to change.

Library of Congress Cataloging-in-Publication Data

Title: Resilience.
Other titles: HBR emotional intelligence series.
Description: Boston, Massachusetts : Harvard Business Review Press, [2017] | Series: HBR emotional intelligence series
Identifiers: LCCN 2016056296 | ISBN 9781633693234 (pbk. : alk. paper)
Subjects: LCSH: Resilience (Personality trait) | Management.
Classification: LCC BF698.35.R47 R462 2017 | DDC 155.2/4—dc23 LC record available at https://lccn.loc.gov/2016056296

ISBN: 978-1-63369-323-4
eISBN: 978-1-63369-324-1

The paper used in this publication meets the requirements of the American National Standard for Permanence of Paper for Publications and Documents in Libraries and Archives Z39.48-1992.

MIX
Paper from responsible sources
FSC® C013056

Contents

Resilience

HBR EMOTIONAL INTELLIGENCE SERIES

1

How Resilience Works

By Diane Coutu

When I began my career in journalism—I was a reporter at a national magazine in those days—there was a man I'll call Claus Schmidt. He was in his mid-fifties, and to my impressionable eyes, he was the quintessential newsman: cynical at times, but unrelentingly curious and full of life, and often hilariously funny in a sandpaper-dry kind of way. He churned out hard-hitting cover stories and features with a speed and elegance I could only dream of. It always astounded me that he was never promoted to managing editor.

But people who knew Claus better than I did thought of him not just as a great newsman but as a

3

quintessential survivor, someone who had endured in an environment often hostile to talent. He had lived through at least three major changes in the magazine's leadership, losing most of his best friends and colleagues on the way. At home, two of his children succumbed to incurable illnesses, and a third was killed in a traffic accident. Despite all this—or maybe because of it—he milled around the newsroom day after day, mentoring the cub reporters, talking about the novels he was writing—always looking forward to what the future held for him.

Why do some people suffer real hardships and not falter? Claus Schmidt could have reacted very differently. We've all seen that happen: One person cannot seem to get the confidence back after a layoff; another, persistently depressed, takes a few years off from life after her divorce. The question we would all like answered is, Why? What exactly is that quality of resilience that carries people through life?

It's a question that has fascinated me ever since I first learned of the Holocaust survivors in elementary school. In college, and later in my studies as an affiliate scholar at the Boston Psychoanalytic Society and Institute, I returned to the subject. For the past several months, however, I have looked on it with a new urgency, for it seems to me that the terrorism, war, and recession of recent months have made understanding resilience more important than ever. I have considered both the nature of individual resilience and what makes some organizations as a whole more resilient than others. Why do some people and some companies buckle under pressure? And what makes others bend and ultimately bounce back?

My exploration has taught me much about resilience, although it's a subject none of us will ever understand fully. Indeed, resilience is one of the great puzzles of human nature, like creativity or the religious instinct. But in sifting through psychological research and in reflecting on the many stories of resilience I've heard, I have seen a little more deeply into the hearts and minds of people like

Claus Schmidt and, in doing so, looked more deeply into the human psyche as well.

The buzz about resilience

Resilience is a hot topic in business these days. Not long ago, I was talking to a senior partner at a respected consulting firm about how to land the very best MBAs—the name of the game in that particular industry. The partner, Daniel Savageau (not his real name), ticked off a long list of qualities his firm sought in its hires: intelligence, ambition, integrity, analytic ability, and so on. "What about resilience?" I asked. "Well, that's very popular right now," he said. "It's the new buzzword. Candidates even tell us they're resilient; they volunteer the information. But frankly, they're just too young to know that about themselves. Resilience is something you realize you have *after* the fact."

"But if you could, would you test for it?" I asked. "Does it matter in business?"

Savageau paused. He's a man in his late forties and a success personally and professionally. Yet it hadn't been a smooth ride to the top. He'd started his life as a poor French Canadian in Woonsocket, Rhode Island, and had lost his father at six. He lucked into a football scholarship but was kicked out of Boston University twice for drinking. He turned his life around in his twenties, married, divorced, remarried, and raised five children. Along the way, he made and lost two fortunes before helping to found the consulting firm he now runs. "Yes, it does matter," he said at last. "In fact, it probably matters more than any of the usual things we look for." In the course of reporting this article, I heard the same assertion time and again. As Dean Becker, the president and CEO of Adaptiv Learning Systems, a four-year-old company in King of Prussia, Pennsylvania, that develops and delivers programs about resilience training, puts it: "More than education, more than experience, more than training, a person's level of resilience will determine who succeeds and who fails. That's true in the cancer ward, it's true in the Olympics, and it's true in the boardroom."

Academic research into resilience started about 40 years ago with pioneering studies by Norman Garmezy, now a professor emeritus at the University of Minnesota in Minneapolis. After studying why many children of schizophrenic parents did not suffer psychological illness as a result of growing up with them, he concluded that a certain quality of resilience played a greater role in mental health than anyone had previously suspected.

Today, theories abound about what makes resilience. Looking at Holocaust victims, Maurice Vanderpol, a former president of the Boston Psychoanalytic Society and Institute, found that many of the healthy survivors of concentration camps had what he calls a "plastic shield." The shield was comprised of several factors, including a sense of humor. Often the humor was black, but nonetheless it provided a critical sense of perspective. Other core characteristics that helped included the ability to form attachments to others and the possession of an inner psychological space that protected the survivors from the intrusions of abusive others. Research about other groups uncovered different qualities associated with resilience. The Search Institute, a Minneapolis-based nonprofit organization that focuses on resilience and youth, found that the more resilient kids have an uncanny ability to get adults to help them out. Still other research showed that resilient inner-city youth often have talents such as athletic abilities that attract others to them.

Many of the early theories about resilience stressed the role of genetics. Some people are just born resilient, so the arguments went. There's some truth to that, of course, but an increasing body of empirical evidence shows that resilience—whether in children, survivors of concentration camps, or businesses back from the brink—can be learned. For example, George Vaillant, the director of the Study of Adult Development at Harvard Medical School in Boston, observes that within various groups studied during a 60-year period, some people became markedly more resilient over their lifetimes. Other psychologists claim that unresilient people more easily develop resiliency skills than those with head starts.

Most of the resilience theories I encountered in my research make good common sense. But I also observed that almost all the theories overlap in three ways. Resilient people, they posit, possess three characteristics: a staunch acceptance of reality; a deep belief, often buttressed by strongly held values, that life is meaningful; and an uncanny ability to improvise. You can bounce back from hardship with just one or two of these qualities, but you will only be truly resilient with all three. These three characteristics hold true for resilient organizations as well. Let's take a look at each of them in turn.

Facing down reality

A common belief about resilience is that it stems from an optimistic nature. That's true but only as long as such optimism doesn't distort your sense of reality. In extremely adverse situations, rose-colored thinking can actually spell disaster. This point was made poignantly to me by management researcher and writer Jim Collins, who happened upon this concept while researching *Good to Great*, his book on how companies transform themselves out of mediocrity. Collins had a hunch (an exactly wrong hunch) that resilient companies were filled with optimistic people. He tried out that idea on Admiral Jim Stockdale, who was held prisoner and tortured by the Vietcong for eight years.

Collins recalls: "I asked Stockdale: 'Who didn't make it out of the camps?' And he said, 'Oh, that's easy. It was the optimists. They were the ones who said we were going to be out by Christmas. And then they said we'd be out by Easter and then out by Fourth of July and out by Thanksgiving, and then it was Christmas again.' Then Stockdale turned to me and said, 'You know, I think they all died of broken hearts.'"

In the business world, Collins found the same un-blinking attitude shared by executives at all the most successful companies he studied. Like Stockdale, resilient people have very sober and down-to-earth views of those parts of reality that matter for sur-vival. That's not to say that optimism doesn't have its place: In turning around a demoralized sales force, for instance, conjuring a sense of possibility can be a very powerful tool. But for bigger challenges, a cool, almost pessimistic, sense of reality is far more important.

Perhaps you're asking yourself, "Do I truly under-stand—and accept—the reality of my situation? Does my organization?" Those are good questions, particularly because research suggests most people slip into denial as a coping mechanism. Facing reality, really facing it, is grueling work. Indeed, it can be unpleasant and often emotionally wrenching. Consider the following story of organizational resilience, and see what it means to confront reality.

Prior to September 11, 2001, Morgan Stanley, the famous investment bank, was the largest tenant in the World Trade Center. The company had some 2,700 employees working in the south tower on 22 floors between the 43rd and the 74th. On that horrible day, the first plane hit the north tower at 8:46 a.m. and Morgan Stanley started evacuating just one minute later, at 8:47 a.m. When the second plane crashed into the south tower 15 minutes after that, Morgan Stanley's offices were largely empty. All told, the company lost only seven employees despite receiving an almost direct hit.

Of course, the organization was just plain lucky to be in the second tower. Cantor Fitzgerald, whose offices were hit in the first attack, couldn't have done anything to save its employees. Still, it was Morgan Stanley's hard-nosed realism that enabled the company to benefit from its luck. Soon after the 1993 attack on the World Trade Center, senior management recognized that working in such a symbolic center of U.S. commercial power made the company vulnerable to attention from terrorists and possible attack.

With this grim realization, Morgan Stanley launched a program of preparedness at the micro level. Few companies take their fire drills seriously. Not so Morgan Stanley, whose VP of security for the Individual Investor Group, Rick Rescorla, brought a military discipline to the job. Rescorla, himself a highly resilient, decorated Vietnam vet, made sure that people were fully drilled about what to do in a catastrophe. When disaster struck on September 11, Rescorla was on a bullhorn telling Morgan Stanley employees to stay calm and follow their well-practiced drill, even though some building supervisors were telling occupants that all was well. Sadly, Rescorla himself, whose life story has been widely covered in recent months, was one of the seven who didn't make it out.

"When you're in financial services where so much depends on technology, contingency planning is a major part of your business," says President and COO Robert G. Scott. But Morgan Stanley was prepared for the very toughest reality. It had not just one but three recovery sites where employees could congregate and business could take place if work locales were ever disrupted. "Multiple backup sites seemed like an incredible extravagance on September 10," concedes Scott. "But on September 12, they seemed like genius."

Maybe it was genius; it was undoubtedly resilience at work. The fact is, when we truly stare down reality, we prepare ourselves to act in ways that allow us to endure and survive extraordinary hardship. We train ourselves how to survive before the fact.

The search for meaning

The ability to see reality is closely linked to the second building block of resilience, the propensity to make meaning of terrible times. We all know people who, under duress, throw up their hands and cry, "How can this be happening to me?" Such people see themselves as victims, and living through hardship carries no lessons for them. But resilient people devise constructs about their suffering to create some sort of meaning for themselves and others.

I have a friend I'll call Jackie Oiseaux who suffered repeated psychoses over a 10-year period due to an undiagnosed bipolar disorder. Today, she holds down a big job in one of the top publishing companies in the country, has a family, and is a prominent member of her church community. When people ask her how she bounced back from her crises, she runs her hands through her hair. "People sometimes say, 'Why me?' But I've always said, 'Why *not* me?' True, I lost many things during my illness," she says, "but I found many more—incredible friends who saw me through the bleakest times and who will give meaning to my life forever."

This dynamic of meaning making is, most researchers agree, the way resilient people build bridges from present-day hardships to a fuller, better-constructed future. Those bridges make the present manageable, for lack of a better word, removing the sense that the present is overwhelming. This concept was beautifully articulated by Viktor E. Frankl, an Austrian psychiatrist and an Auschwitz survivor. In the midst of staggering suffering, Frankl invented "meaning therapy," a humanistic therapy technique that helps individuals make the kinds of decisions that will create significance in their lives.

In his book *Man's Search for Meaning*, Frankl described the pivotal moment in the camp when he developed meaning therapy. He was on his way to work one day, worrying whether he should trade his last cigarette for a bowl of soup. He wondered how he was going to work with a new foreman whom he knew to be particularly sadistic. Suddenly, he was disgusted by just how trivial and meaningless his life had become. He realized that to survive, he had to find some purpose. Frankl did so by imagining himself giving a lecture after the war on the psychology of the concentration camp, to help outsiders understand what he had been through. Although he wasn't even sure he would survive, Frankl created some concrete goals for himself. In doing so, he succeeded in rising above the sufferings of the moment. As he put it in his book: "We must never forget that we may also find meaning in life even when confronted with a hopeless situation, when facing a fate that cannot be changed."

Frankl's theory underlies most resilience coaching in business. Indeed, I was struck by how often businesspeople referred to his work. "Resilience training—what we call hardiness—is a way for us to help people construct meaning in their everyday lives," explains Salvatore R. Maddi, a University of California, Irvine psychology professor and the director of the Hardiness Institute in Newport Beach, California. "When people realize the power of resilience training, they often say, 'Doc, is this what psychotherapy is?' But psychotherapy is for people whose lives have fallen apart badly and need repair. We see our work as showing people life skills and attitudes. Maybe those things should be taught at home, maybe they should be taught in schools, but they're not. So we end up doing it in business."

Yet the challenge confronting resilience trainers is often more difficult than we might imagine. Meaning can be elusive, and just because you found it once doesn't mean you'll keep it or find it again. Consider Aleksandr Solzhenitsyn, who survived the war against the Nazis, imprisonment in the gulag, and cancer. Yet when he moved to a farm in peaceful, safe Vermont, he could not cope with the "infantile West." He was unable to discern any real meaning in what he felt to be the destructive and irresponsible freedom of the West. Upset by his critics, he withdrew into his farmhouse, behind a locked fence, seldom to be seen in public. In 1994, a bitter man, Solzhenitsyn moved back to Russia.

Since finding meaning in one's environment is such an important aspect of resilience, it should come as no surprise that the most successful organizations and people possess strong value systems. Strong values infuse an environment with meaning because they offer ways to interpret and shape events. While it's popular these days to ridicule values, it's surely no coincidence that the most resilient organization in the world has been the Catholic Church, which has survived wars, corruption, and schism for more than 2,000 years, thanks largely to its immutable set of values. Businesses that survive also have their creeds, which give them purposes beyond just making money. Strikingly, many companies describe their value systems in religious terms. Pharmaceutical giant Johnson & Johnson, for instance, calls its value system, set out in a document given to every new employee at orientation, the Credo. Parcel company UPS talks constantly about its Noble Purpose.

Value systems at resilient companies change very little over the years and are used as scaffolding in times of trouble. UPS Chairman and CEO Mike Eskew believes that the Noble Purpose helped the company to rally after the agonizing strike in 1997. Says Eskew: "It was a hugely difficult time, like a family feud. Everyone had close friends on both sides of the fence, and it was tough for us to pick sides. But what saved us was our Noble Purpose. Whatever side people were on, they all shared a common set of values. Those values are core to us and never change; they frame most of our important decisions. Our strategy and our mission may change, but our values never do."

The religious connotations of words like "credo," "values," and "noble purpose," however, should not be confused with the actual content of the values. Companies can hold ethically questionable values and still be very resilient. Consider Phillip Morris, which has demonstrated impressive resilience in the face of increasing unpopularity. As Jim Collins points out, Phillip Morris has very strong values, although we might not agree with them—for instance, the value of "adult choice." But there's no doubt that Phillip Morris executives believe strongly in its values, and the strength of their beliefs sets the company apart from most of the other tobacco companies. In this context, it is worth noting that resilience is neither ethically good nor bad. It is merely the skill and the capacity to be robust under conditions of enormous stress and change. As Viktor Frankl wrote: "On the average, only those prisoners could keep alive who, after years of trekking from camp to camp, had lost all scruples in their fight for existence; they were prepared to use every means, honest and otherwise, even brutal . . . in order to save themselves. We who have come back . . . we know: The best of us did not return."

Values, positive or negative, are actually more important for organizational resilience than having resilient people on the payroll. If resilient employees are all interpreting reality in different ways, their decisions and actions may well conflict, calling into doubt the survival of their organization. And as the weakness of an organization becomes apparent, highly resilient individuals are more likely to jettison the organization than to imperil their own survival.

Ritualized ingenuity

The third building block of resilience is the ability to make do with whatever is at hand. Psychologists follow the lead of French anthropologist Claude Levi-Strauss in calling this skill bricolage.[1] Intriguingly, the roots of that word are closely tied to the concept of resilience, which literally means "bouncing back." Says Levi-Strauss: "In its old sense, the verb *bricoler* . . . was always used with reference to some extraneous movement: a ball rebounding, a dog straying, or a horse swerving from its direct course to avoid an obstacle."

Bricolage in the modern sense can be defined as a kind of inventiveness, an ability to improvise a solution to a problem without proper or obvious tools or materials. Bricoleurs are always tinkering—building radios from household effects or fixing their own cars. They make the most of what they have, putting objects to unfamiliar uses. In the concentration camps, for example, resilient inmates knew to pocket pieces of string or wire whenever they found them. The string or wire might later become useful—to fix a pair of shoes, perhaps, which in freezing conditions might make the difference between life and death.

When situations unravel, bricoleurs muddle through, imagining possibilities where others are confounded. I have two friends, whom I'll call Paul Shields and Mike Andrews, who were roommates throughout their college years. To no one's surprise, when they graduated, they set up a business together selling educational materials to schools, businesses, and consulting firms. At first, the company was a great success, making both founders paper millionaires. But the recession of the early 1990s hit the company hard, and many core clients fell away. At the same time, Paul experienced a bitter divorce and a depression that made it impossible for him to work. Mike offered to buy Paul out but was instead slapped with a lawsuit claiming that Mike was trying to steal the business. At this point, a less resilient person might have just walked away from the mess. Not Mike. As the case wound through the courts, he kept the company going any way he could—constantly morphing the business until he found a model that worked: going into joint ventures to sell English-language training materials to Russian and Chinese companies. Later, he branched off into publishing newsletters for clients. At one point, he was even writing video scripts for his competitors. Thanks to all this bricolage, by the time the lawsuit was settled in his favor, Mike had an entirely different, and much more solid, business than the one he had started with.

Bricolage can be practiced on a higher level as well. Richard Feynman, winner of the 1965 Nobel Prize in physics, exemplified what I like to think of as intellectual bricolage. Out of pure curiosity, Feynman made himself an expert on cracking safes, not only looking at the mechanics of safecracking but also cobbling together psychological insights about people who used safes and set the locks. He cracked many of the safes at Los Alamos, for instance, because he guessed that theoretical physicists would not set the locks with random code numbers they might forget but would instead use a sequence with mathematical significance. It turned out that the three safes containing all the secrets to the atomic bomb were set to the same mathematical constant, e, whose first six digits are 2.71828.

Resilient organizations are stuffed with bricoleurs, though not all of them, of course, are Richard Feynmans. Indeed, companies that survive regard improvisation as a core skill. Consider UPS, which empowers its drivers to do whatever it takes to deliver packages on time. Says CEO Eskew: "We tell our employees to get the job done. If that means they need to improvise, they improvise. Otherwise we just couldn't do what we do every day. Just think what can go wrong: a busted traffic light, a flat tire, a bridge washed out. If a snowstorm hits Louisville tonight, a group of people will sit together and discuss how to handle the problem. Nobody tells them to do that. They come together because it's our tradition to do so."

That tradition meant that the company was delivering parcels in southeast Florida just one day after Hurricane Andrew devastated the region in 1992, causing billions of dollars in damage. Many people were living in their cars because their homes had been destroyed, yet UPS drivers and managers sorted packages at a diversion site and made deliveries even to those who were stranded in their cars. It was largely UPS's improvisational skills that enabled it to keep functioning after the catastrophic hit. And the fact that the company continued on gave others a sense of purpose or meaning amid the chaos.

Improvisation of the sort practiced by UPS, however, is a far cry from unbridled creativity. Indeed, much like the military, UPS lives on rules and regulations. As Eskew says: "Drivers always put their keys in the same place. They close the doors the same way. They wear their uniforms the same way. We are a company of precision." He believes that although they may seem stifling, UPS's rules were what allowed the company to bounce back immediately after Hurricane Andrew, for they enabled people to focus on the one or two fixes they needed to make in order to keep going.

Eskew's opinion is echoed by Karl E. Weick, a professor of organizational behavior at the University of Michigan Business School in Ann Arbor and one of the most respected thinkers on organizational psychology. "There is good evidence that when people are put under pressure, they regress to their most habituated ways of responding," Weick has written. "What we do not expect under life-threatening pressure is creativity." In other words, the rules and regulations that make some companies appear less creative may actually make them more resilient in times of real turbulence.

Claus Schmidt, the newsman I mentioned earlier, died about five years ago, but I'm not sure I could have interviewed him about his own resilience even if he were alive. It would have felt strange, I think, to ask him, "Claus, did you really face down reality? Did you make meaning out of your hardships? Did you improvise your recovery after each professional and personal disaster?" He may not have been able to answer. In my experience, resilient people don't often describe themselves that way. They shrug off their survival stories and very often assign them to luck.

Obviously, luck does have a lot to do with surviving. It was luck that Morgan Stanley was situated in the south tower and could put its preparedness training to work. But being lucky is not the same as being resilient. Resilience is a reflex—a way of facing and understanding the world—that is deeply etched into a person's mind and soul. Resilient people and companies face reality with staunchness, make meaning of hardship instead of crying out in despair, and improvise solutions from thin air. Others do not. This is the nature of resilience, and we will never completely understand it.

DIANE L. COUTU is a former senior editor at HBR specializing in psychology and business.

Note

1. See, e.g., Karl E. Weick, "The Collapse of Sense-making in Organizations: The Mann Gulch Disaster," *Administrative Science Quarterly*, December 1993.

Reprinted from *Harvard Business Review*,
May 2002 (product #R0205B).

2

Resilience for the Rest of Us

By Daniel Goleman

There are two ways to become more resilient: one by talking to yourself, the other by retraining your brain.

If you've suffered a major failure, take the sage advice given by psychologist Martin Seligman in the HBR article "Building Resilience" (April 2011). Talk to yourself. Give yourself a cognitive intervention, and counter defeatist thinking with an optimistic attitude. Challenge your downbeat thinking, and replace it with a positive outlook.

Fortunately, major failures come along rarely in life.

But what about bouncing back from the more frequent annoying screwups, minor setbacks, and irritating upsets that are routine in any leader's life? Resilience is, again, the answer—but with a different flavor. You need to retrain your brain.

The brain has a very different mechanism for bouncing back from the cumulative toll of daily hassles. And with a little effort, you can upgrade its ability to snap back from life's downers.

Whenever we get so upset that we say or do something we later regret (and who doesn't now and then?), that's a sure sign that our amygdala—the brain's radar for danger and the trigger for the fight-or-flight response—has hijacked the brain's executive centers in the prefrontal cortex. The neural key to resilience lies in how quickly we recover from that hijacked state.

The circuitry that brings us back to full energy and focus after an amygdala hijack concentrates in the left side of our prefrontal area, says Richard Davidson, a neuroscientist at the University of Wisconsin. He's also found that when we're distressed, there's heightened activity on the right side of the prefrontal area. Each of us has a characteristic level of left/right activity that predicts our daily mood range—if we're tilted to the right, more upsets; if to the left, we're quicker to recover from distress of all kinds.

To tackle this in the workplace, Davidson teamed with the CEO of a high-pressure, 24/7, biotech startup and meditation expert Jon Kabat-Zinn of the University of Massachusetts Medical School. Kabat-Zinn offered the employees at the biotech outfit instruction in mindfulness, an attention-training method that teaches the brain to register anything happening in the present moment with full focus—but without reacting.

The instructions are simple:

1. Find a quiet, private place where you can be undistracted for a few minutes. For instance, close your office door and mute your phone.

2. Sit comfortably, with your back straight but relaxed.

3. Focus your awareness on your breath, staying attentive to the sensations of the inhalation and exhalation, and start again on the next breath.

4. Do not judge your breathing or try to change it in any way.

5. See anything else that comes to mind as a distraction—thoughts, sounds, whatever. Let them go and return your attention to your breath.

After eight weeks and an average of 30 minutes a day practicing mindfulness, the employees had shifted their ratio from tilted toward the stressed-out right side to leaning toward the resilient left side. What's more, they said they remembered what they loved about their work: They got in touch with what had brought them energy in the first place.

To get the full benefit of mindfulness, a daily practice of 20 to 30 minutes works best. Think of it like a mental exercise routine. It can be very helpful to have guided instructions, but the key is to find a slot for the practice in your daily routine. (There are even instructions for using a long drive as your practice session.)

Mindfulness has steadily been gaining credence among hard-nosed executives. There are centers where mindfulness instruction has been tailored to businesspeople, from tony resorts like Miraval Resort in Arizona to programs in mindful leadership at the University of Massachusetts Medical School. Google University has been offering a course in mindfulness to employees for years.

Might you benefit from tuning up your brain's resilience circuitry by learning to practice mindfulness? Among high-performing executives, the effects of stress can be subtle. My colleagues Richard Boyatzis and Annie McKee suggest as a rough diagnostic of leadership stress asking yourself, "Do I have a vague sense of unease, restlessness, or the feeling that life is not great (a higher standard than 'good enough')?" A bit of mindfulness might put your mind at ease.

DANIEL GOLEMAN is a codirector of the Consortium for Research on Emotional Intelligence in Organizations at Rutgers University, coauthor of *Primal Leadership: Leading with Emotional Intelligence* (Harvard Business Review Press, 2013), and author of *The Brain and Emotional Intelligence: New Insights.*

Adapted from content posted on hbr.org
on March 4, 2016.

3

How to Evaluate, Manage, and Strengthen Your Resilience

By David Kopans

Think back to your last off-site meeting. You and the rest of your team likely poured over reports and spreadsheets, facts and figures. Strewn about the table were probably the tools of your trade: reams of data, balance sheets, and P&Ls. Managers understand that clear-eyed analysis—both quantitative and qualitative—is the key to building a resilient business. And yet when it comes to measuring and strengthening our own ability to adapt, grow, and prosper, rarely do we apply the same methodical approach.

But we should. Based on my own experience starting, building, and growing companies, as well as upon decades of research showing the underlying components of personal resilience, I've discovered a few fundamental things you can do to actually evaluate, manage, and strengthen your own resilience in the same way that you would increase the resiliency of your company:

Build up your positivity currency. We can't just print resilience the way countries print money. Individuals must use what I call a "positivity currency" approach that is grounded in actual positive interactions, events, and memories—factors that are known to boost resilience. This currency is only "printed" and stored as assets when we focus on positive things and express gratitude for them. Why? Because maintaining a positive outlook and regularly expressing gratitude are the bullion bars that have real value in backstopping and building resilience.

Research by Robert Emmons of UC Davis, Michael McCullough of the University of Miami, and others clearly shows that they are among the most reliable methods for increasing personal happiness and life satisfaction.[1] Creating such positivity currency can decrease anxiety, reduce symptoms of illness, and improve the quality of your sleep. All of which, of course, lead to greater personal resilience.

Keep records. None of the tools we use to evaluate companies work very well without good record keeping. That's also true when it comes to building individual resilience. When you commit positive interactions, events, and memories to the written word, they register higher value than other non-written forms of positivity currency-based activity, according to research by positive psychology expert Martin Seligman of the University of Pennsylvania.[2] Record your positive currency transactions (by jotting them down in a leather bound journal or a digital equivalent). The data points you record could be as simple as keeping a written tally by category (such as family, friends, or work) in a paper notebook, entering the information into a spreadsheet, or assigning hashtags to items in a digital gratitude journal.

Create a bull market. Financial markets boom when increasing numbers of investors want in. Likewise, our own resilience grows when we encourage positivity buyers to enter the market. It's not a difficult task; positivity is socially contagious. In the research behind their book *Connected: The Surprising Power of Our Social Networks and How They Shape Our Lives*, Harvard's Nicholas Christakis and the University of California, San Diego's James Fowler detail how happiness depends not just on our own choices and actions, but also on those of people who are two or even three degrees removed from us. What this means is by being more positive ourselves, we encourage others to do the same, and this in turn creates a virtuous "reverse run on the bank" positive feedback loop, and our own resilience is increased and strengthened by the actions of others.

Take a portfolio approach. Resilient businesses diversify risk. Accordingly, resilient individuals diversify their positivity currency. They look to increase their overall resilience by evaluating what it is that provides the highest returns across their entire "life portfolio" and then investing more in those areas. Most frequently, these high-return assets come from our lives outside of the office. Indeed, while we may spend the majority of waking hours at work, our job should not be central to our overall positive outlook. In a 2015 report entitled "The Happiness Study" from Blackhawk Engagement Solutions, respondents ranked their jobs eighth out of a list of 12 contributors to overall happiness. Ranking in the top spots were family, friends, health, hobbies, and community.[3] It follows that by generating more positivity currency in those areas, you will increase the ability to bring your best self to work.

Report regularly. Finally, just as regular review of a company's financials is important to building a resilient business, building individual resilience requires regular review of positivity currency data. This review not only enables you to glean insights and take corrective actions, but also to boost your resilience by simply increasing your exposure to positive interactions and expressions of gratitude. As suggested in a famous 2014 experiment conducted by Facebook's data scientists and published in the Proceedings of the National Academy of Sciences of the United States of America, if your news feed skews positive, so will you.[4]

Even if you don't analyze your positivity currency data deeply like a Wall Street quant, just exposing yourself to it on a regular basis will make you more resilient. So find a regular time to celebrate and re-flect on your positivity currency (I do it while I wait for my morning coffee). Make it a habit, and your level of resilience—and that of your friends, family, and coworkers—will rise.

DAVID KOPANS is the founder and CEO of PF Loop, a company that aims to make positive change in the world through software applications and digital services grounded in positive psychology research.

Notes

1. R. Emmons, "Why Gratitude Is Good," *Greater Good*, November 16, 2010, http://greatergood.berkeley.edu/article/item/why_gratitude_is_good; and "Why Practice Gratitude," *Greater Good*, October 31, 2016, http://greatergood.berkeley.edu/topic/gratitude/definition#why_practice.
2. M. E. Seligman et al., "Positive Psychology Progress: Empirical Validation of Interventions," *American Psychologist* 60, no. 5 (July–August 2005): 410–421.
3. "The Happiness Study: An Employee Rewards and Recognition Study," Blackhawk Engagement Solutions,

June 2, 2105, www.bhengagement.com/report/
employee-happiness-study/.

4. A. D. I. Kramer et al., "Experimental Evidence of Massive-Scale Emotional Contagion Through Social Networks," *Proceedings of the National Academy of Sciences of the United States of America* 111, no. 24 (2014): 8788–8790.

Adapted from content posted on hbr.org on
June 14, 2016 (product # H02XDP).

4

Find the Coaching in Criticism

By Sheila Heen and Douglas Stone

F eedback is crucial. That's obvious: It improves performance, develops talent, aligns expectations, solves problems, guides promotion and pay, and boosts the bottom line.

But it's equally obvious that in many organizations, feedback doesn't work. A glance at the stats tells the story: Only 36% of managers complete appraisals thoroughly and on time. In one recent survey, 55% of employees said their most recent performance review had been unfair or inaccurate, and one in four said they dread such evaluations more than anything else in their working lives. When senior HR executives were asked about their biggest performance management challenge, 63% cited managers' inability or unwillingness to have difficult feedback discussions. Coaching and mentoring? Uneven at best.

Most companies try to address these problems by training leaders to give feedback more effectively and more often. That's fine as far as it goes; everyone benefits when managers are better communicators. But improving the skills of the feedback giver won't accomplish much if the receiver isn't able to absorb what is said. It is the receiver who controls whether feedback is let in or kept out, who has to make sense of what he or she is hearing, and who decides whether or not to change. People need to stop treating feedback only as something that must be pushed and instead improve their ability to pull.

For the past 20 years we've coached executives on difficult conversations, and we've found that almost everyone, from new hires to C-suite veterans, struggles with receiving feedback. A critical performance review, a well-intended suggestion, or an oblique comment that may or may not even be feedback

("Well, your presentation was certainly interesting") can spark an emotional reaction, inject tension into the relationship, and bring communication to a halt. But there's good news, too: The skills needed to receive feedback well are distinct and learnable. They include being able to identify and manage the emotions triggered by the feedback and extract value from criticism even when it's poorly delivered.

Why feedback doesn't register

What makes receiving feedback so hard? The process strikes at the tension between two core human needs—the need to learn and grow, and the need to be accepted just the way you are. As a result, even a seemingly benign suggestion can leave you feeling angry, anxious, badly treated, or profoundly threatened. A hedge such as "Don't take this personally" does nothing to soften the blow.

Getting better at receiving feedback starts with understanding and managing those feelings. You might think there are a thousand ways in which feedback can push your buttons, but in fact there are only three.

Truth triggers are set off by the content of the feedback. When assessments or advice seem off base, unhelpful, or simply untrue, you feel indignant, wronged, and exasperated.

Relationship triggers are tripped by the person providing the feedback. Exchanges are often colored by what you believe about the giver (He's got no credibility on this topic!) and how you feel about your previous interactions (After all I've done for you, I get this petty criticism?). So you might reject coaching that you would accept on its merits if it came from someone else.

Identity triggers are all about your relationship with yourself. Whether the feedback is right or wrong, wise or witless, it can be devastating if it causes your sense of who you are to come undone. In such moments you'll struggle with feeling overwhelmed, defensive, or off balance.

All these responses are natural and reasonable; in some cases they are unavoidable. The solution isn't to pretend you don't have them. It's to recognize what's happening and learn how to derive benefit from feedback even when it sets off one or more of your triggers.

Six steps to becoming a better receiver

Taking feedback well is a process of sorting and filtering. You need to understand the other person's point of view, try on ideas that may at first seem a poor fit, and experiment with different ways of doing things. You also need to discard or shelve critiques that are genuinely misdirected or are not helpful right away.

But it's nearly impossible to do any of those things from inside a triggered response. Instead of ushering you into a nuanced conversation that will help you learn, your triggers prime you to reject, counterattack, or withdraw.

The six steps below will keep you from throwing valuable feedback onto the discard pile or—just as damaging—accepting and acting on comments that you would be better off disregarding. They are presented as advice to the receiver. But, of course, understanding the challenges of receiving feedback helps the giver be more effective, too.

1. Know your tendencies

You've been getting feedback all your life, so there are no doubt patterns in how you respond. Do you defend yourself on the facts ("This is plain wrong"), argue about the method of delivery ("You're really doing this by email?"), or strike back ("You, of all people?")? Do you smile on the outside but seethe on the inside? Do you get teary or filled with righteous indignation? And what role does the passage of time play? Do you tend to reject feedback in the moment and then step back and consider it over time? Do you accept it all immediately but later decide it's not valid? Do you agree with it intellectually but have trouble changing your behavior?

When Michael, an advertising executive, hears his boss make an offhand joke about his lack of professionalism, it hits him like a sledgehammer. "I'm flooded with shame," he told us, "and all my failings rush to mind, as if I'm Googling 'things wrong with me' and getting 1.2 million hits, with sponsored ads from my father and my ex. In this state it's hard to see the feedback at 'actual size.'" But now that Michael understands his standard operating procedure, he's able to make better choices about where to go from there: "I can reassure myself that I'm exaggerating, and usually after I sleep on it, I'm in a better place to figure out whether there's something I can learn."

2. Disentangle the "what" from the "who"

If the feedback is on target and the advice is wise, it shouldn't matter who delivers it. But it does. When a relationship trigger is activated, entwining the content of comments with your feelings about the giver (or about how, when, or where she delivered the comments), learning is short-circuited. To keep that from happening, you have to work to separate the message from the messenger, and then consider both.

Janet, a chemist and a team leader at a pharmaceutical company, received glowing comments from her peers and superiors during her 360-degree review but was surprised by the negative feedback she got from her direct reports. She immediately concluded that the problem was theirs: "I have high standards, and some of them can't handle that," she remembers thinking. "They aren't used to someone holding their feet to the fire." In this way, she changed the subject from her management style to her subordinates' competence, preventing her from learning something important about the impact she had on others.

Eventually the penny dropped, Janet says. "I came to see that whether it was their performance problem or my leadership problem, those were not mutually exclusive issues, and both were worth solving." She was able to disentangle the issues and talk to her team about both. Wisely, she began the conversation with their feedback to her, asking, "What am I doing that's making things tough? What would improve the situation?"

3. Sort toward coaching

Some feedback is evaluative ("Your rating is a 4"); some is coaching ("Here's how you can improve").

Everyone needs both. Evaluations tell you where you stand, what to expect, and what is expected of you. Coaching allows you to learn and improve and helps you play at a higher level.

It's not always easy to distinguish one from the other. When a board member phoned James to suggest that he start the next quarter's CFO presentation with analyst predictions rather than internal projections, was that intended as a helpful suggestion, or was it a veiled criticism of his usual approach? When in doubt, people tend to assume the worst and to put even well-intentioned coaching into the evaluation bin. Feeling judged is likely to set off your identity triggers, and the resulting anxiety can drown out the opportunity to learn. So whenever possible, sort toward coaching. Work to hear feedback as potentially valuable advice from a fresh perspective rather than as an indictment of how you've done things in the past. When James took that approach, "the suggestion became less emotionally loaded," he says. "I decided to hear it as simply an indication of how that board member might more easily digest quarterly information."

4. Unpack the feedback

Often it's not immediately clear whether feedback is valid and useful. So before you accept or reject it, do some analysis to better understand it.

Here's a hypothetical example. Kara, who's in sales, is told by Johann, an experienced colleague, that she needs to "be more assertive." Her reaction might be to reject his advice ("I think I'm pretty assertive already"). Or she might acquiesce ("I really do need to step it up"). But before she decides what to do, she needs to understand what he really means. Does he think she should speak up more often, or just with greater conviction? Should she smile more or less? Have the confidence to admit she doesn't know something or the confidence to pretend she does?

Even the simple advice to "be more assertive" comes from a complex set of observations and judgments that Johann has made while watching Kara in meetings and with customers. Kara needs to dig into the general suggestion and find out what in particular prompted it. What did Johann see her do or fail to do? What did he expect, and what is he worried about? In other words, where is the feedback coming from?

Kara also needs to know where the feedback is going—exactly what Johann wants her to do differently and why. After a clarifying discussion, she might agree that she is less assertive than others on the sales floor but disagree with the idea that she should change. If all her sales heroes are quiet, humble, and deeply curious about customers' needs, Kara's view of what it means to be good at sales might look and sound very different from Johann's *Glengarry Glen Ross* ideal.

When you set aside snap judgments and take time to explore where feedback is coming from and where it's going, you can enter into a rich, informative conversation about perceived best practices—whether you decide to take the advice or not.

5. Ask for just one thing

Feedback is less likely to set off your emotional triggers if you request it and direct it. So don't wait until your annual performance review. Find opportunities to get bite-size pieces of coaching from a variety of people throughout the year. Don't invite criticism with a big, unfocused question like "Do you have any feedback for me?" Make the process more manageable by asking a colleague, a boss, or a direct report, "What's one thing you see me doing (or failing to do) that holds me back?" That person may name the first behavior that comes to mind or the most important one on his or her list. Either way, you'll get concrete information and can tease out more specifics at your own pace.

Roberto, a fund manager at a financial services firm, found his 360-degree review process overwhelming and confusing. "Eighteen pages of charts and graphs and no ability to have follow-up conversations to clarify the feedback was frustrating," he says, adding that it also left him feeling awkward around his colleagues.

Now Roberto taps two or three people each quarter to ask for one thing he might work on. "They don't offer the same things, but over time I hear themes, and that gives me a good sense of where my growth edge lies," he says. "And I have really good conversations—with my boss, with my team, even with peers where there's some friction in the relationship. They're happy to tell me one thing to change, and often they're right. It does help us work more smoothly together."

Research has shown that those who explicitly seek critical feedback (that is, who are not just fishing for praise) tend to get higher performance ratings. Why?

Mainly, we think, because someone who's asking for coaching is more likely to take what is said to heart and genuinely improve. But also because when you ask for feedback, you not only find out how others see you, you also *influence* how they see you. Soliciting constructive criticism communicates humility, respect, passion for excellence, and confidence, all in one go.

6. Engage in small experiments

After you've worked to solicit and understand feedback, it may still be hard to discern which bits of advice will help you and which ones won't. We suggest designing small experiments to find out. Even though you may doubt that a suggestion will be useful, if the downside risk is small and the upside potential is large, it's worth a try. James, the CFO we discussed earlier, decided to take the board member's advice for the next presentation and see what happened. Some directors were pleased with the change, but the shift in format prompted others to offer suggestions of their own. Today James reverse-engineers his presentations to meet board members' current top-of-mind concerns. He sends out an email a week beforehand asking for any burning questions and either front-loads his talk with answers to them or signals at the start that he will get to them later on. "It's a little more challenging to prepare for but actually much easier to give," he says. "I spend less time fielding unexpected questions, which was the hardest part of the job."

That's an example worth following. When someone gives you advice, test it out. If it works, great. If it doesn't, you can try again, tweak your approach, or decide to end the experiment. Criticism is never easy to take. Even when you know that it's essential to your development and you trust that the person delivering it wants you to succeed, it can activate psychological triggers. You might feel misjudged, ill-used, and sometimes threatened to your very core.

Your growth depends on your ability to pull value from criticism in spite of your natural responses and on your willingness to seek out even more advice and coaching from bosses, peers, and subordinates. They may be good or bad at providing it, or they may have little time for it—but you are the most important factor in your own development. If you're determined to learn from whatever feedback you get, no one can stop you.

SHEILA HEEN and DOUGLAS STONE are cofounders of Triad Consulting Group and teach negotiation at Harvard Law School. They are coauthors of *Thanks for the Feedback: The Science and Art of Receiving Feedback Well*, from which this article is adapted.

Reprinted from *Harvard Business Review*, January–February 2014 (product #R1401K).

5

Firing Back

*How Great Leaders Rebound
After Career Disasters*

By Jeffrey A. Sonnenfeld and Andrew J. Ward

Among the tests of a leader, few are more challenging—and more painful—than recovering from a career catastrophe, whether it is caused by natural disaster, illness, misconduct, slipups, or unjust conspiratorial overthrow. But real leaders don't cave in. Defeat energizes them to rejoin the fray with greater determination and vigor.

Take the case of Jamie Dimon, who was fired as president of Citigroup but now is CEO of JPMorgan Chase. Or look at Vanguard founder Jack Bogle, who was removed from his position as president of Wellington Management but then went on to create the index fund and become a leading voice for governance reform. Similarly, there's former Coca-Cola president Steve Heyer, who was surprisingly passed over for the CEO position at Coke but then was quickly named head of Starwood Hotels. Most colorful, perhaps, is Donald Trump, who recovered from two rounds of financial distress in his casino business and is admired today both as a hugely successful estate developer and as a producer and star of popular reality TV shows—and of course ran successfully for President of the United States.

These stories are still the exception rather than the rule. F. Scott Fitzgerald's famous observation that there are no second acts in American lives casts an especially dark shadow over the derailed careers of business leaders. In our research—analyzing more than 450 CEO successions between 1988 and 1992 at large, publicly traded companies—we found that only 35% of ousted CEOs returned to an active executive role within two years of departure; 22% stepped back and took only advisory roles, generally counseling smaller organizations or sitting on boards.

But 43% effectively ended their careers and went into retirement.

What prevents a deposed leader from coming back? Leaders who cannot recover have a tendency to blame themselves and are often tempted to dwell on the past rather than look to the future. They secretly hold themselves responsible for their career setback, whether they were or not, and get caught in a psychological web of their own making, unable to move beyond the position they no longer hold. This dynamic is usually reinforced by well-meaning colleagues and even by family and friends, who may try to lay blame in an attempt to make sense of the chaos surrounding the disaster. Sadly, their advice can often be more damaging than helpful.

In every culture, the ability to transcend life's adversity is an essential feature of becoming a great leader. In his influential 1949 book, *The Hero with a Thousand Faces*, anthropologist Joseph Campbell showed us that the various stories of great leaders around the world, in every culture and every era, are all essentially the same story—the "hero myth." This myth is embodied in the life stages of such universal archetypes as Moses, Jesus, Muhammad, Buddha, Aeneas, Odysseus, and the Aztecs' Tezcatlipoca. Transformational leaders follow a path that entails a call to greatness, early successes (involving tough choices), ongoing trials, profound setbacks, and, ultimately, triumph as they reintegrate into society. If Campbell were writing today, he might want to include business leaders in his study, as they must confront similar trials on their way to greatness.

This article is intended to help leaders—or anyone suffering from an unexpected setback—examine their often abrupt fall from grace and to give them a process through which they can recover, and even exceed their past accomplishments. From our 22 years of interviews with 300 fired CEOs and other derailed professionals, our scholarly study of leadership, our consulting assignments, and our own searing personal experiences, we are convinced that leaders can triumph over tragedy, provided they take conscious steps to do so. For a start, they must carefully *decide how to fight back.* Once this crucial decision has been taken, they must *recruit others into battle.* They must then *take steps to recover their heroic status*, in the process proving to themselves and others that they have the *mettle* necessary to *rediscover their heroic mission.*

Few people exemplify this journey better than President Jimmy Carter. After his devastating 1980 reelection loss to Ronald Reagan, Carter was emotionally fatigued. As he told us sometime later, "I returned to Plains, Georgia, completely exhausted, slept for almost 24 hours, and then awoke to an altogether new, unwanted, and potentially empty life." While proud of his achievements—his success in deregulating energy, for example, his efforts to promote global human rights, and his ability to broker peace between Israel and Egypt through the Camp David Accords—post election, Carter needed to move past his sense of frustration and rejection, particularly his failure to secure the timely release of the American hostages in Iran.

Despite his pain and humiliation, Carter did not retreat into anger or self-pity. He realized that his global prominence gave him a forum to fight to restore his influential role in world events. Accordingly, he recruited others into battle by enlisting the enthusiastic support of his wife, Rosalynn, several members of his administration, academic researchers in the sciences and social sciences, world leaders, and financial backers to build the Carter Center. He proved his mettle by refusing to remove himself from the fray. Indeed, he continued to involve himself in international conflict mediation in Ethiopia and Eritrea, Liberia, Haiti, Bosnia, and Venezuela, demonstrating in the process that he was not a has-been. He regained his heroic stature when he was awarded the Nobel Peace Prize in 2002 "for his decades of untiring effort to find peaceful solutions to international conflicts, to advance democracy and human rights, and to promote economic and social development." And he has rediscovered his heroic mission by using the Carter Center to continue his drive to advance human rights and alleviate needless suffering.

Let us look now at how some great business leaders have followed the same path to recover from their own disastrous career setbacks.

Decide how to fight back

The first decision you will face in responding to a career disaster is the question of whether to confront the situation that brought you down—with an exhausting, expensive, and perhaps embarrassing battle—or to try to put it behind you as quickly as possible, in the hope that no one will notice or remember for long. In some cases, it's best to avoid direct and immediate confrontation. Home Depot cofounder Bernie Marcus, for example, decided to sidestep the quicksand of litigation against Sandy Sigoloff, the conglomerateur who fired Marcus from Handy Dan

Home Improvement. Marcus made his battleground the marketplace rather than the courtroom. Thanks to this strategy, he was free to set the historic course for the Home Depot, which now under his successor is approaching $100 billion in sales, with several hundred thousand employees.

Other comeback kids also began with a graceful retreat. Jamie Dimon was sacked as president of Citigroup by then chairman Sandy Weill following 16 years of partnership in building the institution. When he spoke to us and to others, he did not dwell on his disappointment or sense of injustice. Monica Langley in her 2003 book *Tearing Down the Walls* describes what happened when Weill asked Dimon to resign. Dimon was shocked but replied, "You've obviously thought this through, and there's nothing I can do." As he scanned the already-prepared press release, Dimon saw that the board agreed with Weill. The firm offered Dimon a generous, nonrestrictive severance package, so a battle with Weill seemed pointless. While he was unemployed, Dimon read biographies of great national leaders who had truly suffered. He also took up boxing—another way, perhaps, of dealing with the stress and pain. After a year of this, Dimon decided he needed closure, so he invited Weill to lunch at the Four Seasons to thank him. As Dimon recounts in Harvey Mackay's 2004 book, *We Got Fired!*: "I had mellowed by then. Sandy wasn't going to call me. . . . I knew I was ready to say thank you for what he did for me. I also knew he and I should talk about what happened. I wanted to get this event behind me so I could move on. Part of me said I had spent sixteen years with him. Twelve or thirteen were pretty good. You can't just look at one side and not the other. I made my own mistakes; I acknowledged I was partly to blame. Whether I was 40 percent or 60 percent to blame really didn't matter. I felt very good about my meeting with him." In this way, Dimon was able to turn his ouster into an event that yielded both helpful perspective and reassuring resolution. (See the sidebar "Getting Beyond Rage and Denial.")

GETTING BEYOND RAGE AND DENIAL

One of the most important steps on the route to recovery is to confront and acknowledge failure. This
can be as simple as understanding the Machiavellian
politics of others. So as you set about rebuilding your
career, make sure you:

- *Remember that failure is a beginning, not an
  end.* Comeback is always possible.

- *Look to the future.* Preemptive actions are
  often more effective than reactive ones—even
  if they only take the form of standing back and
  reflecting on what to do next.

About six months after that lunch, in March 2000,
Dimon became CEO of Bank One, a huge Chicago
bank that survived the merger of First Chicago and
the original Banc One. That year, Bank One posted a
loss of $511 million. Three years later, under Dimon's

- *Help people deal with your failure.* Even close friends may avoid you because they don't know what to say or do. Let them know that you are ready for assistance and what kind of aid would be most useful.

- *Know your narrative.* Reputation building involves telling and retelling your story to get your account of events out there and to explain your downfall. Be consistent.

leadership, Bank One was earning record profits of $3.5 billion, and its stock price had soared 85%. Adding to the sweetness of vindication, the following year Bank One merged with JPMorgan Chase, an institution with which Weill had long wanted Citigroup to merge. Dimon became CEO of the new company and is now widely regarded as one of the most influential financial executives in the world.

Of course, it's not always a good decision to sit on the sidelines and presume that justice will prevail. The highly respected Nick Nicholas, outmaneuvered as CEO of Time Warner by his skilled rival Gerald Levin, never challenged his old firm. He went off to Vail to ski at the time, awaiting a call back to service, soon becoming a very successful investor in new businesses, a professor, and a board director. But he never regained his role as the leader of a great public enterprise. Other deposed CEOs, such as Ford's Jacques Nasser, Hewlett-Packard's Carly Fiorina, IBM's John Akers, United Air Lines' Richard Ferris, and Apple's John Sculley have similarly failed to return to lead major public firms. They were considered brilliant leaders by many and were never accused of plundering the shareholders' wealth, like some rogue CEOs of recent years. But they never fought back, and they disappeared from the corner office.

The key determinant in the fight-or-flight question is the damage (or potential damage) incurred to the leader's reputation—the most important resource of all leaders. While departed CEOs and other leaders may have enough other resources and experience to rebound, it is their reputation that will make the difference between successful career recovery and failure.

Fights that will result only in a Pyrrhic victory are best avoided. Battles of pure revenge can resemble Shakespearean tragedies, where all parties lose. Hewlett-Packard board member Tom Perkins, for example, in trying to defend his friend and fellow director George Keyworth from allegations of leaking confidential board discussions, not only brought down HP chairman Patricia Dunn but also caused his friend far greater humiliation, forcing him off the board as well. A leader must consider whether fighting the allegations will exacerbate the damage by making the accusations more public.

When, however, the allegations are not only sufficient to cause a catastrophic career setback but would also block a career comeback, then leaders need to fight back. Consider former Israeli prime minister Ariel Sharon. He was a triumphant commander on the Egyptian front in the Six Day War of 1967. Fifteen years later, as minister of defense, Sharon initiated an attack on the Palestine Liberation Organization in Lebanon. Christian militias seized the opportunity to massacre hundreds of Palestinians in acts of revenge against the PLO in the Israeli-controlled Sabra and Shatila refugee camps.

In a February 21, 1983, cover story, *Time* magazine reported that these massacres were the result of a plot between Sharon and the militias to avenge the killing of Lebanon's Christian president Bashir Gemayel. Sharon sued *Time* in Israel and in New York in lengthy litigation. In both places, juries found *Time*'s accusations to be false and defamatory. The magazine settled and apologized. "It was a very long and hard struggle and was worth it," Sharon said publically at the time. "I came here to prove that *Time* magazine lied: We were able to prove that *Time* did lie."

A ferocious warrior, Sharon took on this carefully calculated battle for his reputation and executed it with focus and determination. He knew that if he did not vigorously defend himself, no one else would be able to help him. Sharon could not have regained his honor and returned to public office if he had not challenged these false charges and then moved on with his life.

Recruit others into battle

Whether you fight or tactically retreat for a while, it is essential to engage others right from the start to join your battle to put your career back on track. Friends and acquaintances play an instrumental role in providing support and advice in the process of recovery.

Those who really care for you can help you gain perspective on the good and bad choices you have made. You are also more likely to make yourself vulnerable with those you trust. Without such vulnerability, you cannot hope to achieve the candid, self-critical perspective you will need to learn from your experience. Still, although family and friends can provide invaluable personal support, they may be less effective when it comes to practical career assistance. Research has shown that slight acquaintances are actually more helpful than close friends in steering you toward opportunities for new positions in other organizations.

In an acclaimed study, Stanford University's Mark Granovetter discovered that of those individuals who landed jobs through personal contacts, only 16.7% found them through people they saw at least twice a week; 55.6% found positions through acquaintances seen at least once a year. But 27.8% of job candidates found work through distant acquaintances, whom they saw less than once a year—old college friends, former workmates, or people known through professional associations. In other words, more job contacts will come to you through people you see less than once a year than from people you see twice or more a week. That's because close friends share the same networks as you do, whereas acquaintances are more likely to introduce you to new people and contacts. Indeed, through the power of acquaintance networks, you can reach almost anyone within a few steps. Thus, distant acquaintances that don't appear to have any connection to you may prove key to your recovery when you are trying to get back on your feet.

But it's not enough to have a wide network of acquaintances. The quality of the connections, even the more distant ones, matters as well. That was the case for Home Depot's Bernie Marcus. Marcus was devastated when he was fired as CEO of Handy Dan on what he felt were trumped-up charges made by Sandy Sigoloff, the threatened boss of the parent company, Daylin. "There was a lot of self-pity on my part," Marcus told us. "I was drowning in my sorrow, going several nights at a time without sleeping. For the first time in my adult life, instead of building, I was more concerned with surviving."

Marcus, however, had an unexpected resource. Whether they were close friends and colleagues with whom he worked or acquaintances he dealt with on a casual basis, Marcus treated others with uncommon honesty, respect, and trust. This consideration was reciprocated by people in his network when he needed help; it was one of his less frequent acquaintances, Rip Fleming at Security Pacific National Bank, who made it possible for Marcus to launch Home Depot.

Marcus had raised $2 million in seed money for the Home Depot venture, but that was not enough to get his new company off the ground. He applied to several banks for a line of credit but was turned down every time. Eventually, he knocked at Fleming's door at Security Pacific National. Both Marcus and Fleming believed that the relationship between banker and client should amount to more than just the business transactions they conducted. Consequently, Fleming had become an adviser to Marcus at Handy Dan. Despite these strong professional ties, though, Fleming was initially reluctant to issue a line of credit until Marcus flew out to Los Angeles and sold Fleming on the idea. In the end, Security Pacific National provided a $3.5 million line of credit, which enabled Home Depot to get up and running. Unbeknownst to Marcus, the proposal was repeatedly turned down by the bank's loan committee and was approved only when Fleming marched into the president's office with his resignation letter in hand.

How you build relationships has a huge impact on your prospects for career recovery. Marcus had a way of building relatively strong relationships even in circumstances when most people would settle for weak acquaintanceships. This capacity for affiliation is a litmus test of a leader's ability to bounce back. People who can create connections are much more likely to engender the kind of help they need when fate turns against them.

Recover your heroic status

It's not enough for you to recruit others to advance your career. To launch your comeback, you must actually *do* things to win back the support of a wider audience. To manage this, you must regain what we call your heroic status.

The great leader has a heroic persona that confers a larger-than-life presence. You can achieve this status by developing a personal dream that you offer as a public possession. If your dream is accepted, you achieve renown. If for whatever reason your public vision is ultimately discarded, you suffer the loss of both your private dream and your public identity. After a career disaster, you can rebound only if you are able to rebuild your heroic stature—that is, the public reputation with which you were previously perceived. An intrinsic part of recovering this heroic status involves getting your story out. This calls for a public campaign to educate and inform.

When a CEO is fired, the true causes for the dismissal are often deliberately hidden, as the board seeks to protect the reputation of the firm and itself. The organization often engages in elaborate face-saving activities to disguise the real nature of the exit. Euphemistically, the press reports that the CEO resigned "for personal reasons" or "to spend more time with family." In our interviews with dismissed CEOs, we found that their greatest frustration stemmed from not being able to rebuild their heroic stature by telling their side of the story. We have interviewed several people who had seven-figure separation agreements that were contingent on their toeing the party line when they left. That's a problem when CEOs are publicly sacrificed even though they are not guilty of the accusations that led to their ouster. In such cases, CEOs' inability to challenge and set the record straight can lead to destructive speculation in the press, which can damage their reputations so much that it becomes all but impossible to recover.

Popular wisdom holds that a deposed leader should sign the nondisparagement agreement, accept the noncompete clause, take the money, and run. Our strong belief is that such agreements are a mistake. In the end, your cash will disappear, and you won't be able to get your story out. If you agree not to speak out, be prepared to be unemployed for a number of years.

A lesser-known player in the Enron saga, Daniel Scotto, comes to mind. Scotto was the financial analyst who headed up the research department for the large global investment bank Paribas. Early on, Scotto said that Enron was losing money in all its mainstream businesses and that it was only through offshore finagling that the company was creating the image of profitability. Paribas, which was underwriting a large part of the debt, asked Scotto to recant. When he wouldn't, Paribas put him on an imposed medical leave for three weeks and then fired him. He was forced to sign a nondisparagement agreement that hurt his ability to get his story out. Scotto has been unemployed for five years.

Martha Stewart is the best reminder that it doesn't have to be that way. As the most public example in recent times of a CEO who got her story out, Stewart is a model for how to regain your heroic status. She did it by carefully orchestrating a multitiered campaign to restore her reputation.

The day after she was indicted for obstruction of justice in the federal government's insider-trading investigation of ImClone stock, Stewart took out a full-page advertisement in *USA Today* and the *New York Times* and launched a new website, marthatalks. com. In an open letter to her public, Stewart clearly proclaimed her innocence and her intention to clear her name. She understood intuitively that when a hero stumbles, constituents have to reconcile two conflicting images of the person—the larger-than-life presence the hero once commanded and the hero's new fallen state. In her letter, Stewart managed to eliminate the confusion by making sure that people knew her side of the story. She openly denied any charges of insider trading and hammered home the unreliability of the three witnesses upon which the government based its case. Stewart very proactively helped others continue to believe in her heroic status.

Stewart's open letter was supported by a statement on her website by her attorneys, Robert G. Morvillo and John J. Tigue Jr., who challenged the media to investigate why the government waited nearly a year and a half to file the charges. "Is it because she is a woman who has successfully competed in a man's business world by virtue of her talent, hard work, and demanding standards?" they asked.

With the aid of her attorneys, Stewart ingeniously—and successfully—portrayed herself as a David struggling in a just and valiant quest against the Goliath of government. Her fans, far from abandoning a fallen star, rallied around her. The astounding strength of this sentiment is measured in the stock price of Martha Stewart Living Omnimedia. Even at the midpoint of Stewart's prison sentence, the stock had not merely rebounded—it was 50% higher than before anybody had heard of ImClone and the ill-fated stock transaction. Upon her release from prison, the share price neared an all-time high, ad revenue at her magazines picked up, and she launched two national network TV shows. The more Stewart got her story out, the more loyal her public became.

Stewart managed to provide a reassuring account of what really happened in her case. But what if you can't? What if you have truly stumbled? If you cannot refute the facts of your dismissal because they are so condemning, show authentic remorse. The public is often enormously forgiving of genuine contrition and atonement.

Prove your mettle

Protecting your reputation by knowing how to fight unjust accusations and bringing others on board are both essential precursors to relaunching a career in the aftermath of catastrophe. Ultimately, however, you will recover fully only when you take on that next role or start a new organization. When you show that you can still perform at a credible or superior level, others will begin to think of you as having the mettle to triumph over your career calamity. (See the sidebar "How to Come Back.")

Showing mettle is not easy. Fallen leaders face many barriers on the path to recovery, not least of which are doubts in their own ability to get back to the top. As one fired CEO told us, "I'd never sit here and say, 'Geez, all I have to do is just replicate and do it again.' The chances of doing it again are pretty small." Yet leaders who rebound are unfailingly those who get over this doubt about their ability to do it

HOW TO COME BACK

Our interviews with some 300 derailed CEOs and other professionals, as well as our scholarly leadership research, consulting assignments, and personal experiences, have brought to light five key steps for rebounding from career disaster. Anyone trying to recover from a catastrophic setback can use these steps to match, or even exceed, their past accomplishments.

- *Decide how to fight back.* Pyrrhic victories will hurt you by calling attention to the accusations leveled against you. But when your reputation is unfairly damaged, you must take quick action.

- *Recruit others into battle.* Friends and family can provide comfort and, perhaps, some perspective in your hour of need. But acquaintances may be more important in landing that next job.

(Continued)

- *Recover your heroic status.* Deposed leaders are often advised to sign nondisparagement agreements. Don't do it. Engage instead in a multitiered campaign to clear your reputation and restore your stature.

- *Prove your mettle.* After suffering career disaster, you will probably have doubts about your ability to get back to the top. You must overcome that insecurity and in the process find the courage to prove to others—and yourself—that you have not lost your magic touch.

- *Rediscover your heroic mission.* It is the single-minded pursuit of a lasting legacy that sets great leaders apart. To recover from a disastrous setback, find a new heroic mission that renews your passion and creates new meaning in your life.

again. Even when forced from familiar arenas into totally new fields, some leaders remain unafraid of trying new ventures. This capacity to bounce back from adversity—to prove your inner strength once more by overcoming your shattered confidence—is critical to earning lasting greatness.

Take Mickey Drexler. When Gap founder Donald Fisher poached Drexler away from Ann Taylor in 1983, the Gap was struggling to compete, since it sold the same brands of clothing as everyone else and was caught in a pricing game. Drexler expanded the retailer beyond the core Gap stores to brand extension such as GapKids, babyGap, and GapBody, as well as introducing other complementary brands, including Banana Republic and Old Navy. Between the time he arrived in 1983 and 2000, Gap's sales increased from $480 million to $13.7 billion, and its stock rose 169-fold.

Then things began to go awry. Drexler was accused of having lost his touch as a prescient merchant; suspicion arose in the minds of analysts and in the media that the goods had become too trendy. Although some people have suggested that the real problem was that Fisher's brother had built too many stores too close to one another, Drexler was blamed for the slump, as same-store sales dropped every quarter for two years, and the stock plummeted 75%. On May 21, 2002, Drexler presented the upcoming season's merchandise to the board, confident that he had a great selling line for the fall. It wasn't enough for the directors, and the next morning Fisher fired him, believing that the company was now too large for Drexler's hands-on management style.

Drexler was by this time independently wealthy, but he was nonetheless determined to prove that the failures of the previous two years were not primarily his fault and did not reflect his abilities. He knew that the only way to restore his belief in himself, as well as other people's confidence in him, was to return to a role in which he could once again demonstrate his expertise. He turned down a multimillion-dollar severance package from Gap because it contained a noncompete clause. After he explored a few other avenues, opportunity came knocking in the guise of struggling fashion retailer J.Crew.

With only about 200 stores, J.Crew was a small fraction of the Gap's size and consequently much more amenable to Drexler's hands-on style, giving him a greater opportunity to make an impact. Drexler invested $10 million of his own money to buy a 22% stake in the company from the retailer's private owner, the investment firm Texas Pacific. He took a salary that was less than a tenth of what he had earned at his former employer. "You've no idea how much it's costing me to run this company," he joked in a *New York* magazine article shortly after taking over.

The results more than proved that Drexler still had the right stuff. J.Crew rebounded from a $30 million operating loss in 2003 to an operating profit of over $37 million in 2004. Same-store sales per square foot, one of the key metrics in retailing, rose 18% from $338 to $400, while at his old employer, sales per square foot dropped 3%. By the summer of 2006,

Drexler had increased both sales and profits by 20% and launched a wildly embraced IPO to take J.Crew public. The media celebrated his recovery and acknowledged his obvious talent.

For Drexler, as for others, the comeback required him to prove his worth in a situation that was perceived to be enormously difficult. Start-ups or turnarounds are common contexts in which fallen leaders can recover grace. It is in these demanding situations that leaders find the mettle to prove to themselves and to others that they have not lost their magic touch and that no obstacle is too great to overcome in their quest for return.

Rediscover your heroic mission

Most great leaders want to build a legacy that will last beyond their lifetime. This does not mean having their names etched on an ivy-clad university ediface but rather advancing society by building and leading an organization. This is what we call the leader's heroic mission.

Most of the leaders we have profiled in this article were deeply engaged in building a lasting legacy even before they suffered their career setbacks. It is the loss of this mission that really raises a derailment to catastrophic proportions in the leader's own mind, since it puts at risk a lifetime of achievement. On the day Steve Jobs was fired from Apple in 1985, for example, his friend Mike Murray was so concerned about Jobs's reaction that he went over to Jobs's house and sat with him for hours until Murray was convinced that Jobs would not commit suicide.

Jobs did not wallow in despair for long. A week after his ouster from Apple, he flew to Europe and, after a few days in Paris, headed for the Tuscan hills of northern Italy, where he bought a bicycle and a sleeping bag and camped out under the stars, contemplating what he would do next. From Italy, he went to Sweden and then to Russia before returning home. Once back in California, with his passion and ambition renewed, Jobs set about re-creating himself as a force in the IT world. He went on to found another computer company, NeXT, which Apple purchased in 1996 for $400 million, at which point Jobs returned to Apple and at the same time became the driving force behind the hugely successful computer-graphics studio Pixar. Once back at Apple, Jobs revived and reenergized the company with breakthrough, high-design products, such as the iMac, iBook, and iPod, and took the company into emerging businesses, such as iTunes.

Like Martha Stewart, Steve Jobs was able to recapture his original heroic mission. Other deposed leaders, however, must truly start again because the door to their familiar field is firmly closed, and they must seek new opportunities and create a totally new heroic mission.

That's what Drexel Burnham Lambert financier Michael Milken, the imaginative "king of the junk bonds," had to do. Milken's life was almost the incarnation of the American dream. Born on the Fourth of July, Milken had become a billionaire by his midforties and one of the most influential financiers in the world. Then it all came tumbling down. He was charged with a 98-count criminal indictment, and a massive civil case was brought against him by the SEC for insider trading, stock parking, price manipulation, racketeering, and defrauding customers, among other crimes. He ended up pleading guilty to six relatively minor counts. In November 1990, he was sentenced to 10 years in prison, agreed to pay $600 million at the time, and ended up paying a further $42 million over a probation violation. After serving 22 months, Milken was released early for cooperating with other inquiries. But he was barred from the securities industry for life.

A week later, Milken was diagnosed with prostate cancer and was told he had 12 to 18 months to live. He immediately turned his maniacal zeal into a new heroic mission to conquer this disease. Through aggressive treatment and his own dietary research, he survived to build a huge foundation supporting research to battle prostate cancer. He also created an economic research institute that attracts the world's top scientific, political, religious, and business leaders. Milken still argues that he was wrongly accused. Others may disagree, but few would doubt that he has earned restitution. The public has come to accept that he has paid for his crimes, and there has even been some reconsideration of their actual severity.

It is the single-minded, passionate pursuit of a heroic mission that sets leaders like Steve Jobs and Michael Milken and Jimmy Carter apart from the general population, and it is what attracts and motivates followers to join them. In the worst of cases, to have that life purpose ripped from you and to be prohibited from its further pursuit can leave an unbearable void and doubts as to your reason for being. Finding a new mission to replace your lifelong purpose can be a great struggle, but one that is necessary if you are to recover.

The tragedies and triumphant comebacks of the leaders we have profiled in this article can seem remote, bordering on the mythological, perhaps. But their stories point to important lessons about recovering from career catastrophe. Stunning comeback is possible in all industries, though the challenges vary according to the leadership norms of each field's culture. For example, clergy ensnarled in publicized sex scandals will probably see their careers dissolve, whereas entertainment figures may not only recover but actually benefit from notoriety. Where one profession values trust, another values celebrity. Thus, recovery plans must be adapted to the cultures of different industries.

Whatever the arena in which your recovery takes shape, the important thing to remember is that we all have choices in life, even in defeat. We can lose our health, our loved ones, our jobs, but much can be saved. No one can truly define success and failure for us—only we can define that for ourselves. No one can take away our dignity unless we surrender it. No one can take away our hope and pride unless we relinquish them. No one can steal our creativity, imagination, and skills unless we stop thinking. No one can stop us from rebounding unless we give up.

JEFFREY A. SONNENFELD is the senior associate dean for executive programs, the Lester Crown Professor of Management Practice at the Yale School of Management, and the president of the Executive Leadership Institute at Yale University in New Haven, Connecticut. ANDREW J. WARD is an assistant professor of management at the University of Georgia in Athens, Georgia. This article is drawn from their book of the same title (Harvard Business School Press, 2007).

Reprinted from *Harvard Business Review,*
February 2007 (product #R0701G).

6

Resilience Is About How You Recharge, Not How You Endure

By Shawn Achor and Michelle Gielan

As constant travelers and parents of a 2-year-old, we sometimes fantasize about how much work we can do when one of us gets on a plane, undistracted by phones, friends, and *Finding Nemo*. We race to get all our ground work done: packing, going through TSA, doing a last-minute work call, calling each other, boarding the plane. Then, when we try to have that amazing in-flight work session, we get nothing done. Even worse, after refreshing our email or reading the same studies over and over, we are too exhausted when we land to soldier on with the emails that have inevitably still piled up.

Why should flying deplete us? We're just sitting there doing nothing. Why can't we be tougher—more resilient and determined in our work—so we can accomplish all of the goals we set for ourselves? Through our current research, we have come to realize that the problem is not our hectic schedule or the plane travel itself; the problem comes from a misunderstanding of what it means to be resilient and the resulting impact of overworking.

We often take a militaristic, "tough" approach to resilience and grit. We imagine a marine slogging through the mud, a boxer going one more round, or a football player picking himself up off the turf for one more play. We believe that the longer we tough it out, the tougher we are, and therefore the more successful we will be. However, this entire conception is scientifically inaccurate.

The very lack of a recovery period is dramatically holding back our collective ability to be resilient and successful. Research has found that there is a direct correlation between lack of recovery and increased incidence of health and safety problems.[1] And lack of recovery—whether by disrupting sleep with thoughts of work or having continuous cognitive arousal by watching our phones—is costing our companies $62 billion a year (that's billion, not million) in lost productivity.[2]

And just because work stops, it doesn't mean we are recovering. We "stop" work sometimes at 5 p.m., but then we spend the night wrestling with solutions to work problems, talking about our work over dinner, and falling asleep thinking about how much work we'll do tomorrow. In a study released last month, researchers from Norway found that 7.8% of Norwegians have become workaholics.[3] The scientists cite a definition of "workaholism" as "being overly concerned about work, driven by an uncontrollable work motivation, and investing so much time and effort to work that it impairs other important life areas."[4]

We believe that this definition applies to the majority of American workers (including those who read HBR), and this prompted us to begin a study of workaholism in the United States. Our study will use a large corporate data set from a major medical company to examine how technology extends our working hours and thus interferes with necessary cognitive recovery. We believe this is resulting in huge health care costs and high turnover rates for employers.

Misconceptions about resilience is often bred from an early age. Parents trying to teach their children resilience might celebrate a high school student staying up until 3 a.m. to finish a science fair project. What a distortion of resilience! A resilient child is a well-rested one. When an exhausted student goes to school, he risks hurting everyone on the road with his impaired driving, he doesn't have the cognitive resources to do well on his English test, he has lower self-control with his friends, and at home, he is moody with his parents. Overwork and exhaustion are the opposite of resilience. And the bad habits we learn when we're young only magnify when we hit the workforce.

In her excellent book *The Sleep Revolution*, Arianna Huffington wrote, "We sacrifice sleep in the name of productivity, but ironically our loss of sleep, despite the extra hours we spend at work, adds up to 11 days of lost productivity per year per worker, or about $2,280."

The key to resilience is trying really hard, then stopping, recovering, and then trying again. This conclusion is based on biology. Homeostasis is a fundamental biological concept describing the ability of the brain to continuously restore and sustain well-being.[5] Positive neuroscientist Brent Furl from Texas A&M University coined the term "homeostatic value" to describe the value that certain actions have for creating equilibrium, and thus well-being, in the body. When the body is out of alignment from overworking, we waste vast mental and physical resources trying to return to balance before we can move forward.

As *Power of Full Engagement* authors Jim Loehr and Tony Schwartz have written, if you have too much time in the performance zone, you need more time in the recovery zone; otherwise you risk burnout. Mustering your resources to "try hard" requires burning energy in order to overcome your currently low arousal level. This is called "upregulation." It also exacerbates exhaustion. Thus, the more imbalanced we become due to overworking, the more value there is in activities that allow us to return to a state of balance. The value of a recovery period rises in proportion to the amount of work required of us.

So how do we recover and build resilience? Most people assume that if you stop doing a task like answering emails or writing a paper that your brain will naturally recover, that when you start again later in the day or the next morning, you'll have your energy back. But surely everyone reading this has had times when they lie in bed for hours, unable to fall asleep because their brain is thinking about work. If you lie in bed for eight hours, you may have rested, but you can still feel exhausted the next day. That's because rest and recovery are not the same thing. Stopping does not equal recovering.

If you're trying to build resilience at work, you need adequate internal and external recovery periods. As researchers Fred R. H. Zijlstra, Mark Cropley, and Leif W. Rydstedt write in their 2014 paper: "Internal recovery refers to the shorter periods of relaxation that take place within the frames of the workday or the work setting in the form of short scheduled or unscheduled breaks, by shifting attention or changing to other work tasks when the mental or physical resources required for the initial task are temporarily depleted or exhausted. External recovery refers to actions that take place outside of work—e.g. in the free time between the workdays, and during weekends, holidays or vacations."[6] If after work you lie around on your bed and get riled up by political commentary on your phone or get stressed thinking about decisions about how to renovate your home, your brain has not received a break from high mental arousal states. Our brains need a rest as much as our bodies do.

If you really want to build resilience, you can start by strategically stopping. Give yourself the resources to be tough by creating internal and external recovery periods. In her upcoming book *The Future of Happiness*, based on her work at Yale Business School, Amy Blankson describes how to strategically stop during the day by using technology to control overworking.[7] She suggests downloading the Instant or Moment apps to see how many times you turn on your phone each day. The average person turns on their phone 150 times every day.[8] If every distraction took only one minute (which would be seriously optimistic), that would account for 2.5 hours of every day.

You can use apps like Offtime or Unplugged to create tech free zones by strategically scheduling automatic airplane modes. In addition, you can take a cognitive break every 90 minutes to recharge your batteries. Try to not have lunch at your desk, but instead spend time outside or with your friends—not talking about work. Take all of your paid time off, which not only gives you recovery periods but raises your productivity and the likelihood of promotion.[9]

As for us, we've started using our plane time as a work-free zone and thus as time to dip into the recovery phase. The results have been fantastic. We are usually tired already by the time we get on a plane, and the cramped space and spotty internet connection make work more challenging. Now, instead of swimming upstream, we relax, meditate, sleep, watch movies, journal, or listen to entertaining podcasts. And when we get off the plane, instead of being depleted, we feel rejuvenated and ready to return to the performance zone.

SHAWN ACHOR is the *New York Times* best-selling author of *The Happiness Advantage* and *Before Happiness*, and a popular TED talk, "The Happy Secret to Better Work." He has lectured or researched at over a third of the *Fortune* 100 companies and in 50 countries, as well as for the NFL, Pentagon, and White House. Shawn is leading a series of courses on "21 Days to Inspire Positive Change" with the Oprah Winfrey Network. MICHELLE GIELAN, a national CBS News anchor turned University of Pennsylvania positive psychology researcher, is now the best-selling author of *Broadcasting Happiness*. She is partnering with Arianna Huffington to research how transformative stories fuel success.

Notes

1. J. K. Sluiter, "The Influence of Work Characteristics on the Need for Recovery and Experienced Health: A Study on Coach Drivers," *Ergonomics* 42, no. 4 (1999): 573–583.
2. American Academy of Sleep Medicine, "Insomnia Costing U.S. Workforce $63.2 Billion a Year in Lost Productivity," *ScienceDaily*, September 2, 2011.
3. C. S. Andreassen et al., "The Relationships Between Workaholism and Symptoms of Psychiatric Disorders: A Large-Scale Cross-Sectional Study," *PLoS One* 11, no. 5 (2016).
4. C. S. Andreassen et al., "Psychometric Assessment of Workaholism Measures," *Journal of Managerial Psychology* 29, no. 1 (2014): 7–24.
5. "What Is Homeostasis?" *Scientific American*, January 3, 2000.

6. F. R. H. Zijlstra et al., "From Recovery to Regulation: An Attempt to Reconceptualize 'Recovery from Work'" (special issue paper, John Wily & Sons, 2014), 244.

7. A. Blankson, *The Future of Happiness* (Dallas, Texas: BenBella Books, forthcoming 2017).

8. J. Stern, "Cellphone Users Check Phones 150x/Day and Other Internet Fun Facts," *Good Morning America*, May 29, 2013.

9. S. Achor, "Are the People Who Take Vacations the Ones Who Get Promoted?" *Harvard Business Review* online, June 12, 2015.

Adapted from content posted on hbr.org,
June 24, 2016 (product #H02Z3O).

Index

How to be human at work.

HBR's Emotional Intelligence Series features smart, essential reading on the human side of professional life from the pages of *Harvard Business Review*. Each book in the series offers uplifting stories, practical advice, and research from leading experts on how to tend to our emotional well-being at work.

Harvard Business Review Emotional Intelligence Series

Available in paperback or ebook format. The specially priced six-volume set includes:

- Mindfulness
- Resilience
- Influence and Persuasion

- Authentic Leadership
- Happiness
- Empathy